FACT FINDERS

Educational adviser: Arthur Razzell

Birds of Prey

Joe Firmin

Illustrated by
Richard Hook, Eric Jewell and John Sibbick
Designed by Faulkner/Marks Partnership

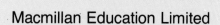

Macmillan Education Limited

100560

© Macdonald Educational 1980

Adapted and published in
the United States by
Silver Burdett Company,
Morristown, N.J.
1980 Printing

ISBN 0-382-06361-9

Library of Congress
Catalog Card No. 80-50426

Birds of Prey

What is a Bird of Prey?

Birds of prey catch and eat birds, animals, snakes, fish and insects. They have hooked beaks and strong claws. Some, called vultures, feed on dead meat.

There are over 400 different kinds of birds of prey in the world. Many live in the African bush where there is plenty of food to catch.

Egyptian vulture

African fish eagle

African fish eagle

Egyptian vultures

Black kite

White-backed vultures

Secretary bird

White-backed vultures

Chanting goshawk

Secretary bird

Eagle

Eagles circle around and can land and turn quickly.

Falcon

Falcons can fly very swiftly after their prey.

Goshawk

Hawks fly fast between trees while hunting.

Each kind of bird of prey has a special shape of wings and tail. The shape affects the way each kind of bird flies.

Falcons, like the kestrel on the right, have narrow pointed wings. They can fly swiftly after their prey. They spread their tails out like a fan when they hover.

Turkey vulture

Vultures (above) use their broad wings to soar and glide. Owls have short wings covered in special soft feathers. The feathers help them to fly silently.

A kestrel hovering

This photograph shows how a little owl moves its wings in flight.

How Birds of Prey Hunt

Ospreys (below) catch fish and
hold them in both feet. Each foot
has two claws facing forwards
and two facing backwards. There are
spiky scales under the toes to help
grasp the slippery prey.

Wood pigeon

Osprey

Fish

Peregrine falcon

Peregrine falcons (left) dive after their prey at great speed. They can knock small birds out of the sky with their talons. Hobbies (below) catch and eat insects while they are flying.

Hobby

Dragonfly

African fish eagle

Most birds of prey eat big meals but they do not eat very often. They use their hooked beaks to tear their food into small pieces.

Fish eagles (above) kill several fish in a day. African secretary birds feed on snakes. They stamp on their prey to kill them. Snail kites have special sharp beaks to eat snails.

White-backed vultures

Carcass

Kestrel

Kestrels (above) eat mice, rats, voles and small birds. Undigested fur, feathers and bones are passed out through their beaks in round pellets.

Vultures (left) eat all but the big bones and skin of large animal carcasses. A flock of vultures like this can pick a carcass clean in only an hour.

Nests and Eggs

Birds of prey lay fewer eggs than most other birds. Eagles usually lay two (right) but not every year.

An eagle's nest is called an eyrie. Sometimes eyries are huge. One nearly two metres wide was once found. It was made of more than a tonne of sticks.

Golden eagle eggs

Golden eagle

Eyrie

Some birds of prey use old nests built by other birds. Sometimes sparrowhawks (above) use old squirrel nests (called dreys) as a base to build their own nests.

Hen harriers (right) build their nests on the ground. Owls lay white, round eggs in holes in trees or in buildings.

Hen harrier and young

Migration

Most birds of prey migrate. They stay in northern countries in the summer. When it gets cold they fly south to warmer areas where they can find food more easily.

Sometimes the birds are shot down as they fly south (below). Many birds are trapped and sold. Only a few countries protect birds of prey.

Viewing tower

Hen harrier

Buzzard

Harrier

Migration routes

You can see the migration routes of the birds of prey on the map below. Thousands of birds fly through the points where the routes meet. Birdwatchers gather to see the birds as they rest and feed (left).

Occasionally the birds are blown off their normal route. The eagle below has wandered off its path.

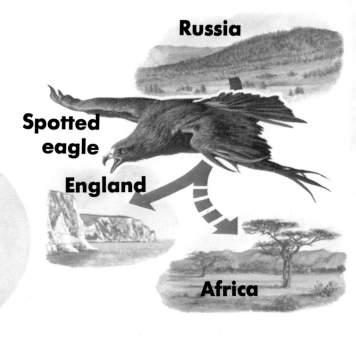

Russia

Spotted eagle

England

Africa

Owls

Little owl

Owls usually hunt at night. They have very good eyesight which helps them see their prey.

On moonless nights owls find their prey by listening to sounds. They have special discs on their faces which trap noise. Their ears help too. They are in different positions on each side of the owl's head.

Snowy owl and chicks

Barn owl and prey

Falconry

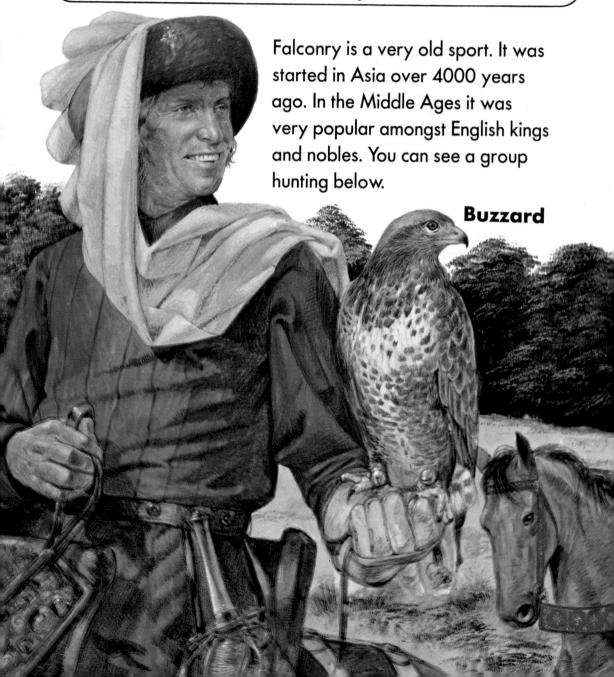

Falconry is a very old sport. It was started in Asia over 4000 years ago. In the Middle Ages it was very popular amongst English kings and nobles. You can see a group hunting below.

Buzzard

The Arabs have always been skilled falconers. They train and fly Saker falcons (right) to kill bustards and other desert game birds.

In Central Asia golden eagles are used to hunt and kill wolves and foxes. In India falcons are used to catch partridges. Good falconry birds are expensive.

Saker falcon

Hooded falcon

Rare Birds of Prey

Some kinds of birds of prey are very rare. Many have been shot, poisoned or trapped. Forests in which they live have been cut down. There are less than 100 monkey-eating eagles left in the Philippines (left).

Spanish Imperial eagle

There are only 100 Spanish Imperial eagles (above) alive today.

Galapagos hawks (right) are naturally tame birds. This makes them easy to catch or shoot. Man has killed so many in the past that there are now only 130 pairs left.

Monkey-eating eagle

Galapagos hawks

Glossary

Bush   Wild and rough country with very few trees. Most of the plants that grow there are small bushes or shrubs.

Carcass   The body of a dead animal.

Discs   A disc is flat, thin and circular in shape. The discs on an owl's face are circles of feathers which help to trap sounds.

Eyrie   The nest of an eagle or a large bird of prey.

Falconry   The art of training birds of prey to catch and kill birds and animals.

Migrate   To move from one place to another. Certain types of bird migrate regularly. When it is cold the birds fly to warmer countries where it is easier for them to find food. They often fly many thousands of miles when they migrate.

Pellets   Small round balls of matter. The pellets which birds of prey expel through their beaks are made of a mass of undigested fur, bones and feathers.

Prey   An animal that is killed and eaten by another animal. When one animal preys upon another it seeks the animal out and kills it.

Soar   To fly high and glide in the air.

Stoop   The fast dive of a falcon on its bird, bat or insect prey.

Talons   Long, sharp claws. Birds of prey use their talons for grasping and killing their prey.

100560

Photo credits: Heather Angel; Frank V. Blackburn; Bruce Coleman Ltd.; Brian Hawkes; Geoffrey Kinns; National History Photographic Agency; Natural Science Photos.

1 2 3 4 5 6 7 8 9 10— R —85 84 83 82 81 80